PIRATES

Grosset & Dunlap

For Sam Rowe—D.A.

For Oren and Elena—D.C.

Text copyright © 1997 by Dina Anastasio. Illustrations copyright © 1997 by Donald Cook. All rights reserved. Published by Grosset & Dunlap, a division of Penguin Young Readers Group, 345 Hudson Street, New York, NY 10014. GROSSET & DUNLAP is a trademark of Penguin Group (USA) Inc. Published simultaneously in Canada. Printed in the U.S.A.

Library of Congress Cataloging-in-Publication Data

Anastasio, Dina.
   Pirates / by Dina Anastasio; illustrated by Donald Cook.
     p. cm.—
   Summary: Describes the life of a pirate, the codes by which pirate crews lived and how they operated, and mentions famous pirates and their lost treasures.
   [1. Pirates.] I. Cook, Donald, ill. II. Title. III. Series.
   G535.A5 1997
     910.4'5---dc20
                                                          96-17597
                                                            CIP

ISBN 0-448-41494-5   H I J   AC

PIRATES

By Dina Anastasio
Illustrated by Donald Cook

Grosset & Dunlap, Publishers

It is a quiet morning on the Caribbean Sea. The year is 1718, and a Spanish ship is sailing over the gentle waves. It is carrying gold, silver, and beautiful jewels back to Spain from the rich New World—America.

Little do the Spanish sailors know, but on the other side of the island, another ship is waiting. It is a pirate ship!

As long as there have been ships to carry treasure across the seas, there have been pirate ships to rob them.

This pirate captain has a plan. He will trick the Spanish ship. He raises a Spanish flag and slowly steers his ship into view. The Spanish captain thinks the ship is friendly, so he does not sail away.

When the pirates are close enough to the Spanish ship, the pirate captain calls to his men, "Hoist the Jolly Roger!"

A black-and-white flag slides up the mast, and the Spanish sailors panic. The flag is a signal. "We are pirates!" it says. "Surrender or be sorry!"

The skull and crossed swords on the flag show that this ship belongs to greedy "Calico Jack" Rackham. Other pirates had their own special Jolly Rogers, too.

The Spanish ship starts firing, but the pirates fire back with cannonballs and smoke bombs.

The pirate ship is smaller and faster and carries more guns. Does the slow, heavy Spanish galleon stand a chance?

No! Soon two cannonballs chained together fly through the air. They break the big mast of the galleon in two. Now the Spanish sailors cannot even sail away.

The pirates swing ropes with hooks onto the deck and quickly climb aboard.

They are a colorful and frightening sight, waving sharp cutlasses and dressed in bright silk scarves, silver buckles, gold, and jewels—all taken from other sailors on other ships.

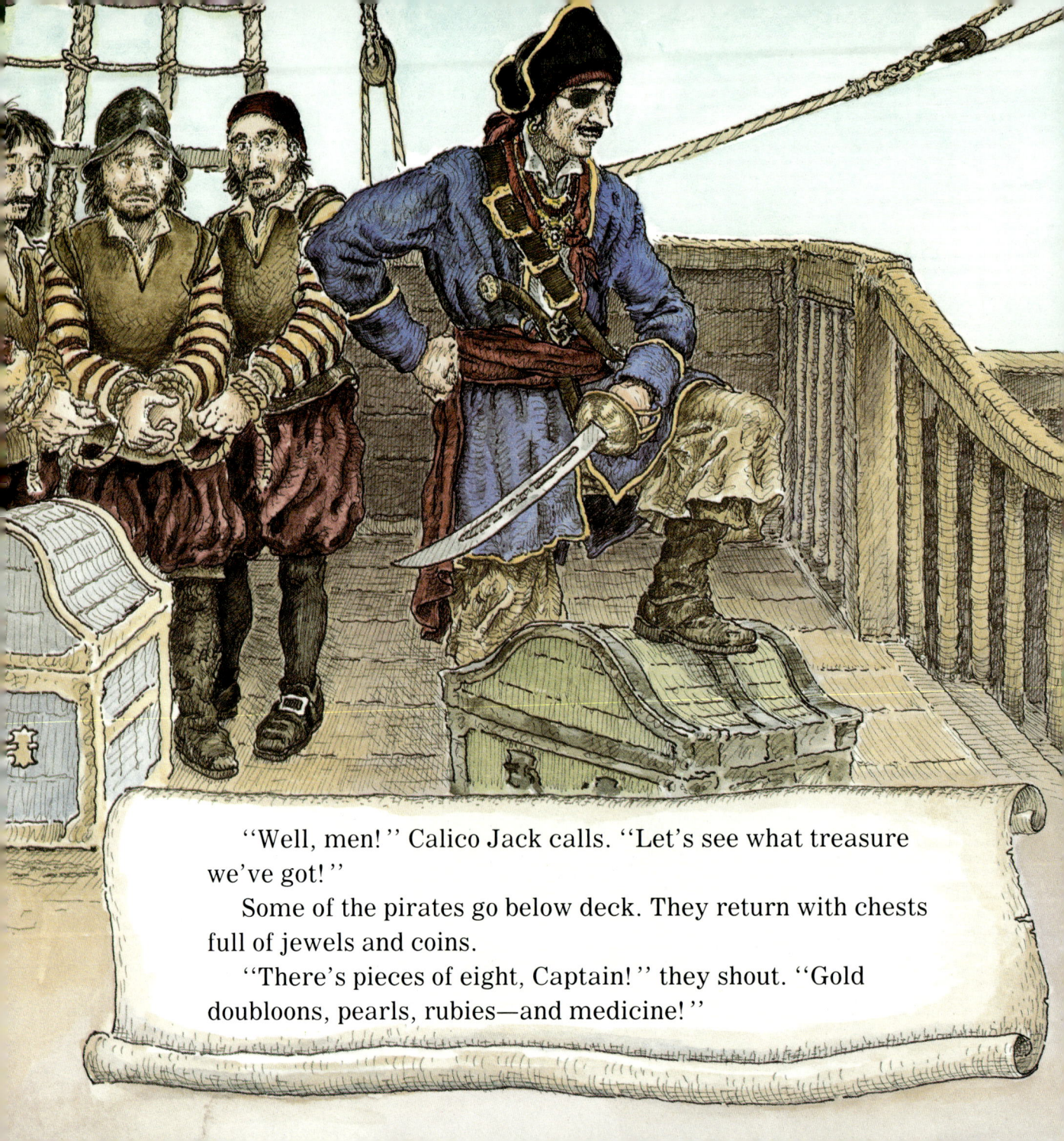

"Well, men!" Calico Jack calls. "Let's see what treasure we've got!"

Some of the pirates go below deck. They return with chests full of jewels and coins.

"There's pieces of eight, Captain!" they shout. "Gold doubloons, pearls, rubies—and medicine!"

Money and jewels are not the only kinds of treasure the pirates are after. They have been at sea for a very long time, and some are sick and hungry. To them, food and medicine are as valuable as gold.

The pirates take all they can from the ship, and burn what they can't carry. Then they sail away to divide up the loot. Each pirate gets an equal share—except for the captain, who gets more. It is part of the pirates' code.

Although they were thieves and murderers, many pirate crews made up their own strict laws to live by. Some even wrote them down. This is how one pirate code might have looked.

Code of Conduct

All crew members shall get an equal share of treasure.
The captain shall get twice as much.
The captain shall be elected fairly.
Everyone shall have an equal vote.
No gambling aboard ship.
While at sea, lanterns and candles must be out at eight o'clock.
Stealing from crewmates and deserting will be punished.

If a pirate broke his ship's code, he was punished. For a small crime, like gambling, a pirate might be fined. But a pirate who did something worse, such as stealing from his shipmates, was in big trouble! Then he was marooned—he was taken to a deserted island and left there with nothing but a jug of water.

What did a pirate do when he was not robbing ships and counting up his loot? He waited at sea for the next ship to rob! Sometimes he waited for weeks and weeks. Then a pirate's life was pretty boring.

Most of the time was spent repairing the ship—patching up ripped sails and mending the lines. The pirates also had to catch their dinner. If they didn't find any fish, they would have to eat hard, wormy biscuits and warm beer.

The best time for pirates came *after* they had robbed a ship. Then they returned to shore to celebrate. Port Royal, Jamaica, was one of the favorite hangouts of the pirates of the Caribbean.

There they ate and drank, gambled and acted as wild as they could, until their treasure was spent and it was time to steal some more.

Of course, not all pirates spent every bit of their loot. The famous pirate Blackbeard is said to have buried lots of his treasure. He was going to come back for it later, but he was captured before he could.

Blackbeard's real name was Edward Teach, and he was one of the meanest pirates ever to set sail. His long, black, bushy beard was tied up with colored ribbons. He wore six pistols, and if that didn't make him look fierce enough, he stuck long matches under his hat and set them on fire to make himself look *more* frightening.

Many treasure hunters have searched for Blackbeard's hidden loot, but no one has ever found it.

Other pirates are said to have buried treasure, too. One of the most famous is Captain Kidd. They say he buried his fortune somewhere on Gardiner's Island, near Long Island, New York, almost three hundred years ago.

The pirate Benito Bonito of the Bloody Sword also left behind a treasure. Today it is called the Lost Loot of Lima. Some say it is still buried on an island off South America. The island's nickname is "Treasure Island." But that fortune, too, has never been found.

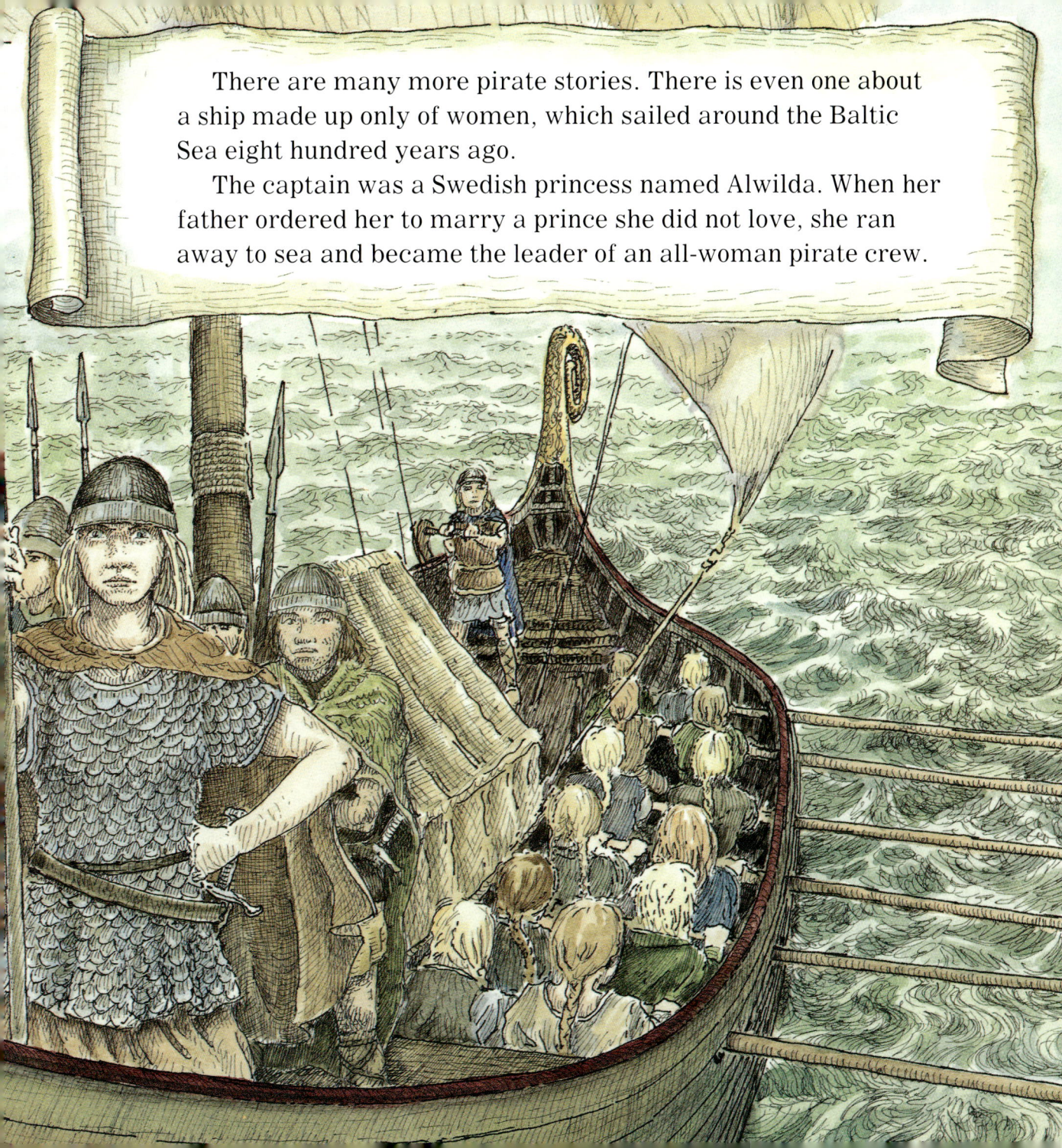

There are many more pirate stories. There is even one about a ship made up only of women, which sailed around the Baltic Sea eight hundred years ago.

The captain was a Swedish princess named Alwilda. When her father ordered her to marry a prince she did not love, she ran away to sea and became the leader of an all-woman pirate crew.

Usually, women weren't allowed on pirate ships. But there were two women in Calico Jack's crew. Anne Bonny and Mary Read dressed up in men's clothes so that neither their prisoners nor their shipmates would know who they really were.

When Calico Jack finally discovered he had women on his crew, he kept their secret, too. Anne and Mary were two of his bravest pirates, and he did not want to lose them.

Today, ships still carry treasures across the oceans, but they are much faster and stronger now, and have better ways of guarding their riches. Luckily, the dangerous days of pirates are over. Still, everyone loves to hear stories about the wild robbers of the seas.